BUS COMPANY
TRAINING VEHICLES

MALCOLM BATTEN

AMBERLEY

First published 2020

Amberley Publishing
The Hill, Stroud
Gloucestershire, GL5 4EP

www.amberley-books.com

Copyright © Malcolm Batten, 2020

The right of Malcolm Batten to be identified
as the Author of this work has been asserted in
accordance with the Copyrights, Designs and
Patents Act 1988.

ISBN 978 1 3981 0097 8 (print)
ISBN 978 1 3981 0098 5 (ebook)

British Library Cataloguing in Publication Data.
A catalogue record for this book is available from
the British Library.

Orgination by Amberley Publishing.
Printed in the UK.

Introduction

The larger bus operators, whether municipal or company owned, have traditionally trained their own new drivers 'in house' rather than relying on commercial companies to provide training. London Transport, the largest bus operator in the country, went a step further, putting all their new drivers through skid training on their purpose-built skid pan at Chiswick Works. Normally older vehicles from the fleet are retained and adapted for training, adorned with 'L' plates. In earlier days they would usually just retain fleet livery. Sometimes they might receive a separate livery or lettering to warn other road users. When the National Bus Company introduced corporate liveries of red or green for its fleets, many of their constituent companies used yellow for their training and service vehicles.

Double-deck vehicles seem to have featured more as trainers than single-deckers, albeit in some fleets (particularly local authority fleets) they formed the bulk of vehicles owned. Until the late 1950s, the classic front-engined half-cab double-decker, normally with a rear platform entrance, was the staple of most fleets, and so these became the choice for training buses. From the late 1950s rear-engined double-deck buses such as the Leyland Atlantean and later Daimler Fleetline began to appear, but not all fleets adopted these and some continued to buy front-engined half-cab 'deckers as well. When this was happening in the 1960s, until production of half-cab double-deckers ceased at the end of the decade, these buses increasingly came to be specified with front entrances. The instructor needed to be able to communicate with the trainee driver. When front engine, half-cab buses with rear entrances were used the bulkhead window behind the driver's cab might be replaced with a sliding panel, or on permanent trainers removed altogether. However, when these half-cab buses became increasingly fitted with front entrances and staircases, this created a new problem. Usually the staircase would be removed and a raised seat for the instructor installed in its place. A window would be fitted in place of the blank panel where the stairs had been. The upper deck seats were often removed as well as they were no longer accessible. When rear-engined buses such as the Leyland Atlantean or Bristol VR came to be cascaded down as trainers the same situation could apply if a front-mounted staircase had been fitted, but the instructor could also occupy the entrance platform alongside the driving position. Where a dual entrance/exit and central staircase were fitted, the situation became easier and there would already often be a window behind the driving position.

Some companies had training buses fitted with dual controls so that the instructor could take over in a potentially dangerous situation. Others might supply the instructor's position with an emergency brake control.

Although double-deck buses used to predominate, single-deck buses and coaches have been used as well, and even minibuses at the time in the 1980s and 1990s when these were all the rage. The vehicles used for training have, of course, become newer as the fleets modernised. So, today's trainers will be low floor, accessible, and usually rear-engined buses as is the required norm for passenger stage services nowadays.

For many years the licence you got and the vehicles you could then drive depended on the type of vehicle on which you took your test. For instance, a test on a single-decker with an automatic gearbox only permitted you to drive similar vehicles. For an 'all-types' licence you needed to pass your test on a manual gearbox double-deck vehicle, and this was considered the most prized type of licence to have.

As the maximum permitted legal length of buses grew longer, the regulations were changed so that there was no separate requirement for driving single or double deck vehicles, but drivers had to take their tests on vehicles at least 9 m (29-ft 6-in.) long.

Rather surprisingly, companies often bought in buses for training from other companies rather than converting their own. Even more surprisingly these might well be chassis types that did not otherwise feature in their fleets, perhaps brought in for the need to have a vehicle with a manual gearbox when their own had all been withdrawn. Therefore, you might get buses like the iconic Southdown 'Queen Mary' Leyland PD3s turning up as a trainer with a company that had no Leyland buses of their own. When the National Bus Company was formed on 1 January 1969 it had brought together the already nationalised Transport Holding Company (THC) fleets, and the former British Electric Traction (BET) fleets. The THC fleets had been largely required to buy Bristol chassis with Eastern Coach Works (ECW) bodywork – both of these companies had come with the nationalisation of the THC fleets and were restricted to selling to nationalised bus companies until 1968. The BET fleets mainly chose AEC or Leyland as their main suppliers. Under the NBC, fleets of THC and BET ancestry were merged, such as Alder Valley comprised of Thames Valley (THC) and Aldershot & District (BET). Vehicles were also cascaded between various fleets so that there became more variety in fleets that had formerly been largely standardised. This extended to training vehicles.

When recruitment became more difficult from around the 1980s, colourful liveries with invitational recruitment slogans (and sometimes stating the potential wages that could be earned) tended to appear and this has continued since. Recruitment was particularly a problem in London, where there was a variety of alternative well-paid work without the unsociable hours associated with working in public transport. Also, after deregulation in the 1980s, some companies began to become more commercial and provide training services generally, not just to their own recruits.

This book looks at a variety of training vehicles from around the country over the last fifty years, including many examples that have survived into preservation. Some of the buses that survived as trainers when others of their type were sold for scrap have been returned to bus format and livery in preservation.

The pictures have been selected to show a wide variety of the more interesting vehicle types and liveries that have appeared during this period.

All photographs are by the author.

A lot of these photographs were taken in the 1970s and 1980s when attitudes were different. Many garages had open access and you could often walk around them unchallenged. If you were, an "Is it OK to take a few pictures around the yard?" would usually be answered in the affirmative. But then came terrorism and health and safety legislation and in came security fencing and CCTV cameras. Photographers motives began to be viewed with suspicion. Some companies, for example South Yorkshire PTE, even tried to ban photography in their bus stations for a time.

Added to this, many town centre bus garages have been sold off for redevelopment as offices, shopping malls or housing and replaced by secure sites on industrial estates. Many bus stations have been rebuilt so that passengers do not need to cross (and are therefore banned from) the areas where vehicles are moving, so creating new challenges for photographers.

So, remember that bus garages are private property and should not be accessed without prior permission. Luckily there are now far more bus rallies, running days and Open Days where there are legitimate opportunities for photographers.

1969–1979

The oldest driver training vehicle I ever encountered was this 1939-built AEC Regent with Park Royal bodywork from the Salford City Transport fleet, photographed in Salford bus station on 4 September 1969. Salford would become part of Selnec PTE (South East Lancashire & North East Cheshire) from 1 November 1969, along with most of the other municipal fleets in the Greater Manchester area. The bus survived into preservation with the Museum of Transport at Manchester. Note the message on the blind display – Dual Control Vehicle.

At the Southampton garage of Hants & Dorset in January 1972 was this Bristol K5G No. 1116. The chassis dated from 1946, but its lowbridge fifty-three-seat body dated from 1940. It had been a training vehicle since 1964.

Gosport & Fareham, trading as Provincial, were an independent operator who sold out to the National Bus Company in January 1970. They had an ageing fleet which included buses on Guy chassis, some rebuilt with Deutz engines and rebodied. Not so modified was this training bus, a Guy Arab III with Duple body that had started life with Red & White in 1949 as their L1949. Seen at Gosport bus station on 22 March 1973, by which time it was in a yellow training livery.

At the Stoke-on-Trent garage of Potteries on 15 May 1974 is T646 (NEH 466). This is a 1949 Leyland OPD2/1 (export model) that was rebodied in 1954 with a Northern Counties lowbridge body, i.e. with an offside sunken gangway on the upper deck. Note the NBC style fleetname. This is another vehicle that has fortunately subsequently passed into preservation with the Potteries Omnibus Preservation Society.

It was not just double-deck buses that were used for training. Midland Red were unique in that they used to design and build their own buses and coaches. KHA 327 was a BMMO C1 of 1949 with Duple C30C body. It was seen on 28 August 1974 leaving the Leicester Corporation Abbey Park Road garage after an Open Day held there to mark fifty years of motorbuses. Although this vehicle did not survive, two other coaches of this design live on in preservation.

The West Midlands PTE was formed in 1969 from a merger of the Birmingham, Walsall, West Bromwich and Wolverhampton Corporation fleets. 131L (ODH 89) was a 1950 Guy Arab III with full-front Park Royal bodywork from the Walsall fleet and still in the corporation blue livery. Taken in Walsall, September 1971.

London Transport bought 4,825 of the AEC RT type between 1939 and 1954 although they were never all in service at any one time. By the 1970s some were in use as trainers while others remained in passenger service until the last route was converted in 1979. Here RT2880, dating from 1952 and with a Park Royal body, is in the forecourt of Potters Bar garage on 23 June 1977. Note advertising for Red Bus Rover tickets, 1,700 miles for 90p, and for the Round London Sightseeing Tour. The RT also displays the customary 'Private – to hire a bus ...' blinds.

A total of 484 RTs passed to the new London & Country company when the country area and Green Line operations were hived off to the National Bus Company from 1 January 1970. RT4490, dating from 1953 and with a Park Royal body, is seen on training duties at Windsor on 2 July 1975. It is in LT dark green livery but carries the London Country 'flying Polo' emblem on the staircase.

We think of driver training, but in the days of half-cab buses there were also conductors. In fact, one-person operation of double-deck vehicles was not legalised until 1966. Although conductors also needed training, a dedicated bus for this was rare. This former Bristol LS coach, now numbered 9095, was in the Southampton garage yard in February 1973. It had possibly been introduced in connection with the changeover to decimal currency in 1971. Hants & Dorset would retain conductors until the last Bristol Lodekkas left the fleet in 1980.

Bristol Omnibus W136, a 1951 Bristol K with highbridge ECW bodywork, was proclaiming itself to be an Engineering Training Unit when it appeared as an exhibit at the Weymouth Rally held on 1 July 1973.

The oldest vehicles in the Portsmouth fleet in 1972 were 1952 Leyland-bodied Leyland PD2/10s. The batch had originally run from GTP 975–999. The doyen of the class was still in service as a trainer when seen in November.

Midland General 15 DRB, a 1958 Bristol LD6B at Nottingham in July 1971. Compared to the vehicles seen so far, this is quite a recent vehicle, at only thirteen years old, to have been downgraded as a full-time trainer. The Midland General group comprised Midland General, Mansfield District and Notts & Derby.

Another trainer in the Potteries fleet at Stoke on Trent on 15 May 1974 (see p. 7) was L679 (203 BEH). This was a 1957 Leyland PD2/20 with Willowbrook L27/28R body that had come into the fleet from Baxter, Hanley. This bus was less fortunate and did not survive into preservation.

Alder Valley was formed in January 1972 when former THC fleet Thames Valley was merged with ex-BET fleet Aldershot & District. While Thames Valley had purchased the customary Bristol/ECW combination, Aldershot & District patronised the local manufacturer, Dennis. SOU 456 is a Dennis Loline 1 of 1958 with East Lancs bodywork. Alder Valley initially adopted a maroon and cream livery but soon changed to National red, which SOU 456 was carrying at Aldershot garage in July 1975.

Representing the ex-Thames Valley part of Alder Valley, and taken at their Reading Garage, are this pair of Bristol LD6G Lodekkas. On the left MBL 844 was former Thames Valley 761 of 1956 while JCY 992 was formerly No. 794, new in 1954 to United Welsh as their 1245.

A pair of South Wales 1958 Bristol LD6G trainers at Swansea garage in February 1976. 260 HNU had started out as Midland General No. 475, while OCY 959 had come from United Welsh when that fleet was merged into an enlarged South Wales company in January 1971.

Eastern National 0976 (976 DHK), a 1955 Bristol LD5G in Southend garage, April 1976.

Another Eastern National Bristol LD5G trainer, No. 0048 (48 PPU), is about to turn into Colchester bus station. 21 July 1976.

Islwyn Borough Transport was the new name for the West Monmouthshire Omnibus Board from January 1974 following the local government changes. MWO 709 was a 1955 Leyland Tiger Cub PSUC1/1 with Weymann body, by now a trainer. Alongside is No. 29 (OAX 160F), a 1968 Leyland Leopard PSU4/1R with Willowbrook body. Both are at the Blackwood garage in April 1976.

A trio of Leyland PD2s inside the garage of Preston Corporation on 15 May 1976. The oldest on the right, No. 57 of 1954, with Leyland bodywork has been relegated to training duties. The other pair date from 1955 and have Metro-Cammell bodywork.

East Kent and Maidstone & District were placed under common management within the National Bus Company. Former East Kent 1962 AEC Regent V YJG 814 became a trainer with M&D at Maidstone garage, seen in July 1976.

A pair of training buses with East Midland at Chesterfield in July 1976. T2 (WAL 123) was a 1957 Leyland PD3/4 with Weymann body; T3 (133 BRR) was an early Leyland Atlantean PDR1/1 of 1959, also with Weymann bodywork.

In the Chesterfield Corporation garage on the same day No. 255 (3255 NU), a 1963 Weymann-bodied Daimler CC6G, was in use for training.

A pair of Northern General training buses at South Shields in July 1976. DT11 (GCN 788) was a 1957 Leyland Tiger Cub PSUC1/1 with Weymann body; AFT 926 was a 1958 Leyland PD3/4 with Weymann body. This had come from the Tynemouth fleet, absorbed in January 1975.

Promotional liveries to attract recruits are more associated with the 1980s onwards, but Hants & Dorset had this attractively painted vehicle on the road back in 1976 when it was photographed in Southampton garage yard. KMW 109 was a 1954 Bristol LD6G acquired with the Wilts & Dorset fleet.

At Southport in September 1976, Merseyside PTE's KFY 30 was a 1954 Leyland PD2/20 with Weymann body from the former municipal fleet. Converted to open-top, it looks as though it doubled up as a tree lopper as well as trainer. Southport had become part of Merseyside PTE in April 1974.

These full-fronted Leyland PD3 buses were a feature of the Ribble fleet, and many like this example had Burlingham bodywork built locally in Blackpool. No. 1547, dating from 1958, had become a trainer when noted parked in Preston bus station on 15 September 1976.

Standing outside the Lincoln Corporation garage in June 1977, KVL 684 was a 1957 Leyland PD2/31 with Roe bodywork.

Full-fronted bodywork was specified for many years by Blackpool Corporation and the vehicles visible in this picture all have this feature. At the Rigby Road garage in July 1977, 360 (YFR 360) is a 1962 Metro-Cammell-bodied Leyland PD3/1. This and the bus to its left have brackets for a slot-in board, as 360 is carrying. Note the PD3A trainer partly visible on the right. This has wasp stripes around the blind box – something more associated with British Railways diesel shunters.

In April 1974 SELNEC PTE gained Wigan and was renamed Greater Manchester PTE. Acquired at the outset in 1969 from Oldham Corporation was 5336 (PBU 936), a 1958 Leyland PD2/20 with Roe body. This had become a trainer when photographed at the Oldham garage in July 1977.

The AEC Routemasters which had passed from London Transport to London Country, on its formation in 1970, were bought back by LT later in the 1970s as London Country replaced then with one-person-operated vehicles. While the RMLs would go into normal passenger service, the RMC class, originally built for Green Line work, did not. These were employed as training vehicles or staff buses, often retaining the green liveries they were acquired in. RMC1508 is seen passing Shepherds Bush market in April 1978.

The RMCs (and initially also RCLs) worked in training duties alongside the RTs until these were all withdrawn. A rather battered RMC1491 stands alongside RT2926 as they take a layover break at Waterloo on 24 June 1978. Note that they both carry adverts for drivers – recruitment was becoming more problematical.

Twenty of these Ribble Burlingham-bodied Leyland PD3s were acquired by London Country, for training purposes in 1975/6, to replace the aging ex-London RTs. 1958-built LR18 was parked up at London Transport's Uxbridge garage on 17 April 1978.

Earlier we saw a Guy Arab trainer for Provincial in 1973. On a visit to their Hoeford garage in June 1978 this 1962 Bristol FS was in use, seen along with one of the company's many Leyland Nationals. XPM 48 had originally been Brighton Hove & District 48, then Southdown 2048, then Hants & Dorset 3496. Both Provincial and Hants & Dorset names are carried – although the companies had separate identities and liveries, they had a common management.

So far we have seen no Bristol single-deck buses as driver trainers in National Bus Company fleets. Western National TU3 (MOD 956) was an early (1953) Bristol LS5G in such use and recorded at Weymouth in July 1978.

Earlier on we saw a conductor training vehicle with Hants & Dorset (see p. 10). Equally unusual and from the same fleet was this bus proclaiming itself as a 'One Person Operator training vehicle'. One-person operation of single-deck vehicles had been common for years and was legalised on double-deck vehicles from 1966. H&D had no double-deck buses suitable for such work until 1971 and would retain conductors on Bristol Lodekkas until 1980. The vehicle seen here at the 1978 Southsea Rally is a 1965 Leyland Panther PSUR1/1R with Willowbrook body ex-Maidstone & District. H&D took thirty-three newer similar vehicles into their fleet from M&D in 1972.

Exeter Corporation sold out to their neighbours Devon General in April 1970. Former Exeter 53, a 1957 Guy Arab IV with Massey body, became Devon General 253 and was being used for training when seen in Torquay during July 1978.

Provincial/Hants & Dorset XPM 48 is seen again in August 1978, but this time at Southampton. Like many NBC trainers it was painted in yellow.

OK, it's another Lodekka, but this is one of the rarer FL 30-foot models. T1 (20 AAX) in the National Welsh fleet had been inherited from Red & White where it was new as L2060 in 1961. Taken at Bristol Rally, 1978.

Glasgow Corporation were one of the original operators of the Leyland Atlantean when these came on the market in 1958. They would subsequently build up a large fleet of these with Alexander bodywork. By May 1979, 1965-built LA282 had become a trainer as seen here. A more modern example of the type follows behind.

At the Halfway garage, inherited with the business of Booth & Fisher, South Yorkshire PTE M108, was a former Sheffield Leyland Atlantean from 1965 which carries bodywork by Neepsend. Neepsend Coachworks Ltd were a short-lived subsidiary of East Lancashire Coachbuilders based in Sheffield, who built bodies to East Lancs design between 1964 and 1968. Taken in May 1979.

Hartlepool is not the sort of place you would normally associate with open-top buses, but they did have this 1958 Leyland PD2/40 with Roe body. It seems to have doubled as a training bus when not otherwise employed. May 1979.

Seen in the gloom of Doncaster's North bus station in May 1979 was this South Yorkshire PTE Leyland PD2 that had come from the local Doncaster fleet. The chassis dated from 1963, but the body dated from 1955 having been originally mounted on a trolleybus until Doncaster dispensed with this mode of transport in December 1963. This vehicle survives at the South Yorkshire Transport Museum.

Northern General T271 was a Marshall-bodied Leyland Leopard PSU3/1R that had originally been Sunderland District 343. It was passing through Stanley, Co. Durham in June 1979.

Seen in the yard of Bishop Auckland garage, United 103 (JNU 986D) was a well-travelled Bristol FLF6G, having previously been Trent 723 and originally Midland General 723. Taken in June 1979.

Taken in Exeter bus station in 1979, Devon General 284 was a 1962 Leyland PD2A/30 with Massey body that had come with the acquisition of Exeter Corporation. This was probably not a full-time training bus as the 'L' plate is a board hung on the front over the radiator filler cap.

Warrington 85 (3713 ED), a 1962 Leyland PD2/40 with East Lancs body. Taken in September 1979.

While training buses were common, a specific bus for recruitment was something of a rarity. But London Transport adapted SMS441, a 1971 AEC Swift with Park Royal body, for this purpose. It was present at an Open Day at West Ham garage on 14 July 1979. This garage later closed in 1992.

1980–1989

PROGRESS back from London Country by London Transport, were deployed as staff or training buses. However, while the shorter RMCs would continue in this role, twenty-six of the RCLs would be modified for service use on route 149 later in 1980, with the rear doors and luggage racks removed and the twin headlights replaced by single ones. This view shows RCL2234 in training use at Bexleyheath garage at the end of 1979.

Looking very smart is Alder Valley 1110, a 1964 Bristol FLF6G formerly Thames Valley D6. This is fitted with coach seating for its original duties on the London–Reading service. Note how the staircase has been removed and an instructor's seat and window installed in its place. Taken at Reading garage, May 1980.

Bristol W163 (837 CHU), formerly bus 8481, was a trainer painted blue and prominently lettered as such when parked in Gloucester bus station in May 1980. It was a 1958 Lodekka LD6G model with, of course, ECW bodywork.

We have seen double-deckers in Bristol's training fleet already. Here is W157, a 1960 Bristol MW5G bus in the customary blue livery, at the 1980 Bristol Rally.

Plymouth favoured Leylands and here is one of their Leyland PD2s in use as their trainer. HJY 297 carried Leyland bodywork and dated from 1953. It was still looking in very fine condition when passing along Royal Parade in May 1980, and it is therefore not surprising that this passed into preservation.

AA (Dodds, Troon) GSD 779, a 1955 Guy Arab IV with Roe rear-entrance body, was in use as a trainer at their depot in May 1980. By this time the main operational fleet had eliminated half-cab double-deckers, as was also the case with their neighbours A1 Services.

East Yorkshire were an NBC ex-BET company who favoured AEC products and CKH 780C was a 1965 AEC Renown with Park Royal bodywork. It had become a trainer when seen at Hull in the company of standard NBC purchases. Taken in June 1980. Note the tapered in upper deck – a feature of EYMS buses for many years to enable them to fit through the medieval arch of Beverley Bar.

Western National TV8 (4386 LJ) was a 1962 Bristol FS6G with ECW body that had been Hants & Dorset No. 1128. It was noted in Torquay on 11 May 1981.

Lincolnshire DT4 was a 1965 Bristol F5G demoted to training and seen in Lincoln on 12 May 1982. Note that both this and Western National TV8 have had new cast fleet number plates made when renumbered for their new role.

Stockport became part of the Greater Manchester PTE at is formation in 1969. They never bought any rear-engined double-deckers, standardising on the Leyland PD2 and later PD3 models. Some of their PD2s are seen as trainers with Greater Manchester in the former Manchester Hyde Road garage. 5840 is in training livery, while 5830 retains fleet livery. Taken in May 1981.

Southampton built up a fleet of over 170 East Lancs-bodied Leyland Atlanteans from 1968 to 1982. No. 122 of 1969 had become a trainer and was on show at the 1981 Southsea Rally.

Nearby Portsmouth Corporation had also updated their training fleet, and on the same day No. 86 (LRV 978), a 1956 Leyland PD2/12 with Metro-Cammell body, was entered in the Southsea Rally, held on the seafront Common. Others of this batch of buses had been converted to open toppers in the early 1970s.

Bought for preservation and entered at the 1981 Sandtoft Gathering in 'as acquired' livery, UUA 212 was an ex-Leeds 1955 Leyland PD2/11 with locally built Roe bodywork, which later served as a training bus for West Yorkshire PTE.

Bristol chose a blue livery for their training fleet as we have seen before. Bristol FLF6G W178 was working in its home city here in August 1981.

Inside the former Brighton Hove & District Whitehawk garage at Brighton is Southdown T772 (OCD 772), a Leyland PD2/12 with Park Royal bodywork. Taken on 2 May 1982.

OCD 772 is one of several buses featured in this book that have since passed on into preservation. In this case that was to happen soon after for here we see Southdown 772 restored to former glory at Netley Rally three years later in July 1985.

Working for United at Hartlepool in May 1982, this Lodekka clearly shows how the staircase has been removed and a seat and window for the instructor installed in its place. FPM 74C had started life as Brighton Hove & District No. 74, reaching United via Southdown No. 2074.

A selection of training buses from the Northern General fleet, all taken in Gateshead on the same day in May 1982. T311 (BUF 253C) is one of the popular ex-Southdown 'Queen Mary' Leyland PD3/4s with Northern Counties bodywork. Northern unusually painted their trainers in National green, while the fleet livery was National red.

This was followed by T451 (EFT 649F), a 1968 Daimler Fleetline CRG6LX with Alexander bodywork, formerly Tynemouth & District 294.

Behind this came T491 (JCN 903J) a 1971 Daimler Fleetline also with Alexander bodywork. This has been downgraded to a permanent trainer after a mere eleven years frontline service.

Northern General were a former BET company and so tended to buy AEC or Leyland chassis, as was usual within the BET empire. However, they did have some unusual vehicles including the only AEC Routemasters outside of London and these Leyland Panthers with Marshall Camair bodywork. GCN 845G of 1969 had become a trainer when also photographed at Gateshead in May 1982.

Looking very bright and eye-catching was this training bus of Yorkshire Traction seen passing through Wakefield – in West Riding territory. T4 was a Leyland Leopard PSU3/4R with Marshall DP49F bodywork. Taken in May 1982.

Taken just around the corner from Sheffield bus station, South Yorkshire PTE MT11 was a 1959 Leyland PD3/1 with Roe body, originally 911 in the Sheffield fleet. Taken in May 1982.

You would have thought Alder Valley would have had enough Bristol Lodekkas and Dennis Lolines to meet its training needs, so it is a puzzle why they acquired this former Ribble Leyland Leopard PSU3/1R with Marshall body. Alder Valley also used a red and yellow livery for trainers so was this a trainer elsewhere beforehand and came in these colours? Seen at Reading garage in March 1983.

More typical of Alder Valley was this early Bristol VR seen at Aldershot garage in June 1983. However, LFS 284F was more interesting because it was new to Eastern Scottish in 1968 as AA284, and had come to Alder Valley in 1973 as part of a deal whereby the Scottish Bus Group disposed of all their VRs to NBC companies in exchange for late model Bristol FLFs. Alder Valley received fourteen VRs in total from three different Scottish fleets in 1973/4.

After Midland Red became a member of the National Bus Company, they started to purchase many of the small independent operators in their area. One of these was Harper Bros of Heath Hayes, near Cannock. HBF 679D was a 1966 Leyland PD2A/27 with MCW bodywork new to the company. Midland Red would be split into four geographical companies in September 1981. This bus passed as a trainer to Midland Red East, where it was in use at Leicester in June 1983.

Maidstone & District were an early convert to rear-engined buses, buying Leyland Atlanteans from 1958 onwards and later switching to Daimler Fleetlines. P185, a 1968 Fleetline with Northern Counties body, had become a trainer at Maidstone by 1983. Note that it carries both Maidstone & District and East Kent fleetnames – both fleets had common management under the NBC.

Rhymney Valley 918 (31 SNY) was a 1963 Leyland PD3/4 with Massey lowbridge bodywork. This had been Caerphilly No. 31 before that fleet had been merged with Gelligaer and Bedwas & Machen to form Rhymney Valley, in April 1974. It was appearing at a rally in Cardiff on 26 June 1983.

By 1983 all RTs had left LT service except RT1530, retained as a demonstration bus on the famous Chiswick Works skidpan, on which all drivers were trained. This was in use when an Open Day was held there on 3 July 1983 as part of the fifty years of London Transport celebrations. The normal skid bus at this time was an RMC Routemaster.

The usual skid pan bus was RMC1518, also seen taking its turn on the wet. The Open Day offered the public the unique experience of travelling on the buses (lower deck only) as the drivers demonstrated their skills on the skid pan.

We saw the AEC Routemasters which London Transport had bought back from London Country earlier. As mentioned, the RMC class were employed as training vehicles or staff buses, often retaining the green liveries they were acquired in. RMC1480 is in National green at the Open Day held at Aldenham Works on 25 September 1983. Another example, repainted red, can be seen behind. In those days, adverts were pasted on rather than inserted into framework, and it is evident where the adverts have been removed.

London Transport chose the Daimler Fleetline as its successor to the AEC Routemaster from 1971. However, these soon fell out of favour and many were being sold out of service by the end of the decade. Some were retained as trainers and DMS 1488, an MCW-bodied vehicle from 1973 with a Leyland engine, was in use as such at Hyde Park Corner on 25 May 1983. The garage code 'A' denotes Sutton.

Although several National Bus Company fleets took former London Transport Daimler Fleetlines into their operational fleet, London Country was not one of these. However Former LT DMS631 was obtained as a trainer and is seen here at Crawley in 1980. This had a Leyland engine, so was more compatible with LCBS's large fleet of Leyland Atlanteans.

Wilts & Dorset 9204, a Bristol FLF6G seen at Poole garage on 5 July 1983. Although new to Wilts & Dorset in 1966, from October 1972 until April 1983 it had been owned by Hants & Dorset when the fleets were merged, before being split again to form Wilts & Dorset and Hampshire Bus. Poole and Bournemouth were in the original Hants & Dorset territory, but now came under Wilts & Dorset.

The Nottinghamshire-based Barton fleet was renowned for buying unusual vehicles, often to their own design. Among the variety were a bunch of AEC Regent Vs with Northern Counties lowbridge bodywork incorporating full-fronts, front entrance and wrap-around windscreens. No. 851 had become a training vehicle when it was entered in the 1983 Showbus Rally at Woburn. Fortunately, this bus and at least one other of the type survive in preservation.

We have seen HBF 679D before with Midland Red East in Leicester in 1983 (see p. 42). Midland Red East was renamed Midland Fox from 15 January 1984, and here the bus is seen repainted and with new fleetnames at a rally in June 1984. This is now in preservation with BaMMOT at Wythall.

The large Bristol Omnibus fleet was split from 11 September 1983 when the Cheltenham, Gloucester, Stroud and Swindon areas became Cheltenham & Gloucester. This 1964 Bristol FLF6G trainer, originally bus 7157, passed to the new company. It was an entrant at the Showbus Rally at Woburn on 2 September 1984. The lettering suggests that the company were also doing commercial training as well as for their own staff.

Among the first vehicles ordered by the new London Country Bus Services when it was formed in 1970 were ninety AEC Reliances with Park Royal dual-purpose bodies for Green Line services. RP87 was one of the class, new in 1972. By September 1984, when it was entered in the Showbus Rally at Woburn, it was a permanent trainer. Note how a yellow band has replaced white on its NBC livery and also the 'flying polo' emblem on the front. It carries the WY code for Addlestone garage (Weybridge).

Many bus companies bought London Transport Daimler Fleetlines when they decided to dispose of them prematurely. One of these was Brighton Corporation although they only took two, including former DMS132, a Daimler CRL6 model with Park Royal body dating from 1971. This became a trainer. What it was doing back in London, at Tower Hill on 21 May 1985, is unclear.

Posed at a rally at the Norfolk Showground near Norwich in September 1984, Eastern Counties X66 (GNG 125C) was a 1965 Bristol FS5G, formerly LFS 125. This bus is now preserved at the Ipswich Transport Museum.

Eastern Counties LFS 125 as seen in preservation at the Ipswich Transport Museum in 2016. As can be seen this has been restored in NBC red livery.

The former municipal fleet of Wigan had been absorbed into the Greater Manchester PTE in April 1974. Former Wigan 146 now GMPTE 3270, a 1964 Leyland PD2A/27 with Massey body, had become a trainer when seen at a rally in Fleetwood during June 1985.

As well as the Routemasters bought back from London Country, London Transport also bought the front-entrance Routemasters that had been operated on behalf of British Airways before the Piccadilly Line was extended to Heathrow. Although thirteen of these were used as buses at Romford during 1975/6 (despite having no blind boxes), these and the others soon became trainers or staff buses. RMA 4 was seen at the North Weald Rally in June 1985. Here the public were offered the chance to drive a bus for a small fee, and the instructor can be seen giving instructions, the bulkhead window behind the driver having been removed.

A trio of training buses with London Transport, at the back of Bexleyheath garage in August 1986. RMA65 is seen with DMS1996 and DMS1470 – all looking rather faded.

Former Wilts & Dorset Bristol FLF6G No. 679, in use as a training bus with Provincial, was an entry at the Netley Rally on 7 July 1985.

Also at the July 1985 Netley Rally, the local Hants & Dorset Company entered several vehicles from its service fleet. Among these was 9201 (EMR 288D), another ex-Wilts & Dorset FLF in use as an engineering training bus. To its right can be glimpsed a Bristol LH converted to an information bus. To its left another trainer, probably from the Bristol fleet.

Seen at the Hoeford garage of Provincial are two former Wilts & Dorset Bristol FLF Lodekkas. EMR 292D carries Hampshire Bus livery, while EMR 295D in yellow training livery now sports a revised Provincial fleetname. All these fleets had been under common management until split in 1983. After 1983 Provincial came under common management with Hampshire Bus, though retained a separate identity and livery. Taken in June 1987.

At Ipswich garage, Eastern Counties X67 was a Bristol FLF6G, formerly Eastern National 2717. Taken in August 1985.

At the 1985 Showbus Rally at Woburn, United Counties 1966 Bristol FS6G KBD 717D was a training bus. Alongside is similar KBD 712D, which had been in preservation with the 712 Preservation Group, Luton, since 1981.

Burnley & Pendle was the new name for Burnley, Colne & Nelson, after the local government reforms in April 1974. HHG 25 was a 1959 Leyland Tiger Cub PSUC1/1 with East Lancs bodywork, latterly in use as a trainer. It had passed into preservation when seen here at the 100 years of tramways rally in Blackpool on 29 September 1985.

Southdown will always be remembered for their fleet of 'Queen Mary' Leyland PD3s with full-fronted Northern Counties bodywork. HCD 360E was from the final 1967 batch, which uniquely featured these large panoramic windows giving them a somewhat bizarre appearance. 360 had been demoted to a trainer at Eastbourne when seen in June 1988.

The Southdown 'Queen Marys' were a popular choice for other companies to acquire as trainers. Former Southdown 364 passed to Alder Valley and appears to be freshly repainted here at Aldershot in July 1985.

Former Southdown 365 had travelled a long way from its South Coast homeland to work as trainer NDT2 for Northern Scottish in Aberdeen, where it was spotted in September 1986. Note it still carries the same advertising as No. 360 carried in Eastbourne – I shouldn't think PDH picked up many orders from Scotland!

East Kent had a large fleet of AEC Regent Vs, and MFN 949F is from the final batch bought in 1967. By April 1987 it had become a trainer and was seen inside Ashford garage along with a Leyland National also so employed.

In Liverpool, Merseybus 1174 (XKC 801J), a 1971 Leyland Atlantean with Alexander dual-door bodywork, was seen. Training lettering has been applied to the standard fleet livery. Taken in July 1987.

The Daimler Roadliner was not a particularly successful design, and many of those bought had quite short lives. One company that had more success with these was Darlington Transport. As well as buying Nos 13–60 from 1967–72, they also bought Nos 83–6/90 from Tyne & Wear PTE in 1979. These had been ordered by South Shields. No. 90 became a trainer and was seen at the Sandtoft Gathering in July 1987.

The country area services of Bristol Omnibus were hived off as a separate company – Badgerline – from 1 January 1986. Although no Bristol Lodekkas passed to the new company as part of the bus fleet, this 1963 example transferred as trainer W177. Looking resplendent in its new livery, this was entered in the Bristol Rally in August 1987.

Derby Corporation standardised on Daimler buses, but acquired this former East Kent 1959 AEC Regent V as a trainer. It was part of the original batch of these buses with East Kent, the only batch to have full-front bodywork. It was parked in the bus station (since replaced) in May 1988.

Another bus from the south coast that found its way to Scotland for training. Clydeside Scottish were using FPM 73C, a 1965 Bristol FLF6G originally Brighton Hove & District 73. However, it had previously been a trainer with United as had similar FPM 74C (see p. 38). FPM 73C seems to have been fitted with the older style of radiator grille at some stage. Seen at Paisley, May 1988.

Kingston-upon-Hull 89 HBC was a 1964 Leyland PD3A/1 with East Lancs body acquired from Leicester, where it had been No. 89. As can be seen, KHCT were offering a broad range of general training services, not just training their own drivers. Taken in May 1988.

Another AEC with East Yorkshire, but T1 (BOW 503C) was not new to them. It had come from the fleet of Southampton Corporation where it was No. 366. Seen in Hull in May 1988 it had been treated to the pre-NBC East Yorkshire livery of dark blue and cream and was looking very smart. This is now preserved.

North Devon, trading as Red Bus, was formed when Western National was split up in January 1983. Training bus AJB 550A was a 1963 AEC Regent V with Park Royal body that had started out with East Kent where it had been registered 6803 FN. It was at Exeter in June 1988.

Midland Red West were using HAC 628D, a Leyland Leopard L2 with Marshall DP41F body that had come to Midland Red with the acquisition of Stratford Blue. It was seen at the 1988 Bristol Rally.

HAC 628D is now in preservation and back in Stratford Blue livery. This was it at Leicester Rally in May 1997.

In April 1989 London Buses were split into eleven regional operating units, plus London Coaches who ran the sightseeing services. DMS1872 is seen soon after with Metroline at Edgware garage. It carries the brighter livery with black skirt and white band introduced by Leaside District.

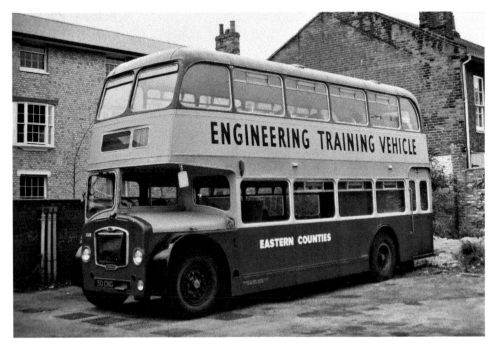

Eastern Counties X68, a Bristol FS5G formerly LFS50, but now lettered as an engineering training vehicle when seen at Ipswich garage in March 1989.

Alder Valley was split into two parts – Alder Valley North and South – from 1 January 1986. From 24 January 1987, Alder Valley North was renamed the Berks Bucks Bus Co. but traded as Bee Line. In April 1989 this Bristol VRTSL26LX with ECW body was in use as trainer T2. It had come from Maidstone & District, where it was fleet No. 5814. It was seen at a rally at Addlestone in April 1989.

London Country was split into four geographical segments from 7 September 1986. London Country South East was then renamed Kentish Bus from 27 April 1987. Neither London Country or its successors ever ran Bristol Lodekkas in passenger service, but Kentish Bus had this ex-Bristol example for training, and it looked very smart in their fleet livery. It was also entered at the Addlestone Rally on 9 April 1989.

Another Kentish Bus trainer was this Park Royal-bodied Leyland Atlantean, new to London Country as AN3 in 1972. Painting over the upper deck windows seems a bit over the top! North Weald Rally, June 1989.

Another Southdown 'Queen Mary' Leyland PD3, but this one was still with Southdown and had been repainted in the traditional pre-NBC livery. It was at the 1989 Southsea Rally. You will not be surprised to learn that this was later preserved – one of many of the type that survive.

At Dewsbury in September 1989, the combined West Riding/Yorkshire fleet were using GHL 193L, a Bristol VRTSL26G, one of the first batch of four for West Riding new in 1972.

On the same day in Huddersfield, Yorkshire Rider 9372 RVH 467N was a 1974 Daimler Fleetline CRG6LX with Roe bodywork. This was one of a batch, RVH 451–68N, ordered by Huddersfield Corporation but delivered new to West Yorkshire PTE after its creation in April 1974. West Yorkshire PTE was renamed Yorkshire Rider in October 1986.

It's another of those ex-Southdown Leyland PD3s; this time with United Counties arriving at the Showbus Rally at Woburn in September 1989. Like many of the Southdown convertible open toppers it had been re-registered so that the original registrations (400–24 DCD batch) could be transferred to coaches, thus not showing their age.

Also sent to Woburn and parked ahead of the PD3 was Luton & District 1027, a former Nottingham City Transport 1965 AEC Renown with Weymann bodywork. Luton & District had been hived off from United Counties in January 1986. The AEC Renown had come with the takeover of Red Rover, Aylesbury, on 30 January 1988.

1990–1999

We are in the 1990s now, and many bus companies were in the height of a mass mania for minibuses. Fitting then that we have a training minibus. Metro was the brand name for Cheltenham & Gloucester's minibuses. One of their Mercedes vehicles can just be seen on the left. The trainer though is a rare Ford AO609, possibly ex-Bournemouth. Taken in Gloucester, May 1990.

We have seen this Southampton Leyland Atlantean before (see p. 35) but note that the fleet has now been rebranded as Citybus. Taken at Southampton in April 1990.

At Edinburgh bus station in May 1990, Eastern Scottish DD56 is an ECW-bodied Daimler Fleetline. Note how the traditional Scottish blindbox has been adapted to display the 'L'.

Privatisation of the National Bus Company has been taking place, and Southdown has become part of the growing Stagecoach empire. Stagecoach stripes now adorn this Leyland PD3 trainer seen at the 1990 North Weald Rally. This is another of the many vehicles of this type that are now preserved.

Two more of the ex-Southdown PD3s, both re-registered. PRX 186B passed to Trent and was at their garage in Derby in July 1990. A preserved ex-Midland General FLF can just be seen on the left.

Provincial 202 (WOW 993T) was one of a pair of the convertible open toppers that were bought from Southdown for seaside use in 1987. By 1992 it had become a trainer and was entered in that year's Southsea Rally. Originally Southdown 423 (423 DCD) this also survives in preservation.

Looking smart but anonymous without lettering, this Bristol FLF of Cheltenham & Gloucester was at an event held at the Science Museum store, Wroughton, near Swindon in September 1990.

London Country South West was formed when London Country was split into four parts in September 1986. From 27 April 1989 they were renamed London & Country to reflect the amount of London-tendered services they had won. This former Blackpool Leyland PD3A with Metro-Cammell body seems an odd choice of trainer. Taken at Addlestone garage, April 1991.

In standard fleet livery, this Southend-on-Sea Corporation Leyland PD3/6 with Massey bodywork had already been bought for preservation when seen here at Canvey Island in April 1991.

We saw former East Kent AEC Regent V PFN 852 earlier when it was working for Derby Corporation in 1988 (see p. 58), 1991 saw it still in use but now with Luton & District and still retaining the livery it carried at Derby. It was entered in the North Weald Rally in June. Although six of this batch of AEC Regents survive, this one did not.

Working for Eastern Counties at Norwich in June 1991 was HCS 806N, a 1975 Leyland Leopard PSU3/3R with Alexander body originally with Western Scottish.

Entering the bus station in May 1992 is Colchester Borough Transport ABN 771V, a Plaxton-bodied Ford coach.

London General Daimler Fleetline THX 476S had been adapted as a training bus numbered DMT2476. On 3 May 1992 I encountered it running in Brighton. It may have been on hire to Brighton & Hove or attending the HCVS London–Brighton run, held on that day, as a tender vehicle.

Retrenchment from the routes running out of the Greater London area, and losses on tendering, had made several of the London BL class of Bristol LH's redundant, so CentreWest adapted some for training use. BL4 was parked outside Paddington station on 25 March 1991. The company's main office was across the road.

Also with CentreWest was RMC1492, seen at the 1993 North Weald Rally. The locations of the company's garages are listed to attract local recruits. The yellow blind reads 'RMC1492 30th anniversary 1962–1992'.

Passing opposite Newcastle station was Northumbria WHN 594M, a 1974 Bristol LH/ECW new to United as 1594. Taken in June 1992.

Another Bristol LH. This one was with Devon General in Exeter during May 1994.

This 1975 LH started with United as No. 1647 then passed to Northumbria. When seen at the 1995 North Weald Rally, it had become a trainer with Stagecoach East Kent.

HUP 441N was new as Northern General 3239 in 1974. When seen at the Gateshead Metrocentre in May 1993 it was trainer T508. This is another company offering general training services; in fact the Northern name is not displayed.

North Weald Rally 1993 and Luton & District No. 1027 has been entered to a rally again. This is not the ex-Nottingham AEC Renown we saw in 1989 but a Plaxton-bodied coach...

The Leyland National was designed as a standard vehicle for NBC companies and was taken by almost all of them, so it is not surprising that some should progress to the training fleets. Also at North Weald in 1993 was Luton & District NPD 113L. This had started out as London Country LN13 – a number it still carries. Originally dual entrance, the centre doors have been panelled over.

Another second-hand Leyland National. KCG 627L had begun life as Alder Valley 127 in 1973 but passed to Trent in 1984 where it later became a trainer. Here it is seen after passing into preservation but before returning to Alder Valley identity.

We saw a former Scottish Leyland Leopard earlier with Eastern Counties. This is Midland Red West with MHS 17P a 1975 bus ex-Central Scottish T239. This was at the Bristol Rally in August 1992.

Passing through the centre of Bradford in June 1992, Yorkshire Rider 9406 has Duple bodywork.

Southend 347, a 1967 Leyland PD3/4 with East Lancashire bodywork, swapped the blue and cream of Southend for the red and cream of Plymouth when it became a trainer in the Devon fleet. It had returned east for preservation when it was entered in the 1995 North Weald Rally.

Thamesway XYK 761T, a 1978 Bedford YLQ with Duple C41F, had started out with George Ewer & Sons (Grey-Green Coaches). Canvey Island, October 1995.

Stagecoach East London T512 lost its roof, probably due to arson, and was converted to open-top. Thereafter it was used for training and private hire, and occasionally in service if there was a shortage of available vehicles. On this occasion in May 1995 it was on training duty in Romford.

From 1984 to 2004 London Buses, and in turn Transport for London, would not allow all-over advertising on service buses. However, this restriction did not apply to buses used only on training duties and some of the privatised companies took advantage of this. Cowie-owned South London was one and these two MCW Metrobuses were entered at the Cobham Gathering held at Brooklands, Woking, in April 1996. This was a short-lived phase – once adverts were once again allowed on service buses they ceased on trainers.

Another Metrobus, this time M147 for London United at Stamford Brook garage in April 1997. Note the prominence placed on the phone number as the way potential applicants should contact the bus company. This was the 1990s and mobile phones had arrived in a big way.

Because of London Transport Buses's red livery stipulation, Stagecoach could not use their national white and stripes livery scheme on their London fleets, but this did not apply to training buses, so here is Selkent Leyland Titan T224. It is passing the former Woolwich Arsenal complex, approaching Plumstead garage with a rather remarkable absence of other road traffic.

Taken at Crowthorne in 1997, CPG 160T was a Plaxton-bodied AEC Reliance with London & Country.

Emerging from Lincoln bus station, Lincolnshire Road Car RDX 11R was a 1976 Leyland Atlantean with Roe bodywork formerly in the Ipswich fleet as No. 11. Taken in May 1997.

We saw a Bristol LH of Northumbria in this same location at Newcastle earlier on. This LH was working for Busways, formerly the Tyne & Wear PTE. It had originated with Eastern Counties as LH929. Taken in August 1997.

Photographed in Oxford, this anonymous training vehicle was with the local Oxford company. VUD 33X, a Leyland Leopard PSU3G/4R, had started life in 1982 with an ECW coach body but was rebodied with a Willowbrook bus body. Taken in May 1998.

Reading Buses training bus No. 200 was a Ford with Duple coach bodywork. Taken in September 1997.

By the end of the 1990s, the bus industry had largely been privatised and had become dominated by major groups – Arriva, First Group, Stagecoach and the Go-Ahead Group. The first three of these had national corporate liveries and here we have a First Manchester bus in a training version of their 'Barbie' livery. G62 RND was present at the Showbus Rally held at Duxford Airfield in September 1999.

Also at Duxford in 1999, Metroline M1393 has not only received an overall orange training livery, the owners have also applied contravision to the windows to further spell out their message.

2000–2019

We start the new millennium with a bunch of London and ex-London vehicles, as this Leyland National 2 was with London General on central London Red Arrow routes until cascaded out to First Beeline at Slough. It had become a training bus when pictured in June 2000.

The same livery style is evident on First Centrewest M1338, at a somewhat deserted Hyde Park Corner on 5 April 2002.

At the Cobham Gathering at Brooklands in April 2002 was this attractively painted Metrobus M1022 of London United. The coach seating is a legacy of its former use on Airbus services.

You can hardly miss the message on Go-Ahead London General NV139! A Volvo Olympian with Northern Counties bodywork, it was heading south along Whitehall during 2004.

The nearside of another London General Volvo Olympian. NV172 (R372 LGH) carries the Northern Counties Palatine II style of bodywork. Taken in April 2005.

Stagecoach East London inherited twenty-six DAF SB220 buses with Optare Excel bodywork built in 1992. A few others were added from other Stagecoach fleets. One of these, 26002, is seen as a trainer in corporate livery alongside 17751, a 2002 Transbus Trident with Alexander ALX400 body, the standard type of double-decker being bought at the time. They are at North Woolwich on 30 May 2003.

The first low floor fully accessible single-deck buses in London were batches of Dennis Lance and Scania buses both with Wrights bodywork, delivered in 1994. Some of the Scanias went to East London, where they were used on route 101. After replacement on this route some became trainers, such as SLW29 or 28629 as it had now become under Stagecoach ownership. This view was taken in 2005.

After the last batch of colourful vehicles, here is a much plainer bus with Arriva. Volvo/Plaxton coach 614 WEH was with Midland Red North and was seen at Crewe in May 2000.

Arriva used this white and grey livery with minimal lettering on some of their trainers. NIW 6511 was a National Greenway, rebodied by East Lancs with Arriva the Shires and taken at a rally in Southend during 2000.

This smart looking Leyland National was with the Milton Keynes operator MK Metro. It was taken at the Brooklands Rally in April 2002.

Back in 1979 we saw a specialised recruiting bus with London Transport. In 2002 we see another, this time with First Essex. Mercedes Benz 709D 9030 was an entrant at a rather wet Showbus Rally at Duxford Airfield.

Stagecoach East Midland 52146, a re-registered Plaxton-bodied Volvo coach became a permanent trainer in this attractive livery utilising aspects of the Stagecoach 'house style'. Taken at Showbus, Duxford, in 2006.

The Dennis Dart in its various guises has been the main single-deck vehicle type for most bus fleets since the 1990s. Therefore, it is not surprising that examples of this type have cascaded into training roles as they have been replaced by newer vehicles. Brighton & Hove J980 JNJ was a 1992 Plaxton-bodied step-entrance model, taken over with the Brighton Corporation fleet in 1997.

Also with Brighton & Hove was R235 HCD, a 1998 Volvo B10BLE with Wright body at the 2008 Worthing Rally. This is one of two of this batch that have since entered preservation, along with many other examples of the modern low floor design of bus.

It's that Arriva white and grey livery again, but this time enhanced with some more lettering. This is not a Dennis Dart but a 1994 Volvo B6 with Plaxton body at the 2011 South East Bus Festival at Detling Showground.

Stagecoach this time. The livery of this Stagecoach Oxford Volvo with Alexander bodywork is a variation on the groups 'swoosh' style that replaced the earlier zigzag stripes. It was taken at a rally at Newbury Showground in July 2012.

Summer 2013 and Yellow Buses, Bournemouth, TB473, a Dennis Dart with East Lancs body, has been colourfully painted for its role as a training vehicle. The former Bournemouth Corporation fleet is now owned by the RATP Group, who have kept the tradition of a yellow-based livery dating back to at least the 1950s.

A Dart from Arriva Medway Towns, but this time it is one of the SLF step-free models with Plaxton Pointer bodywork dating from 1997. This was at the 2014 South East Bus Festival at Detling Showground.

The first low floor double-deck buses to enter service in London arrived in 1998 and were DAF DB250LF models with Alexander ALX400 bodies for Arriva. The first, DLA1, had become a trainer by 2014 and this photo was taken at the RM60 Routemaster event in Finsbury Park on 13 July 2014. Given the historical significance of this vehicle I imagine it will eventually be retained as part of their heritage fleet.

There are now buses built in the present millennium that have been downgraded to serve as permanent trainers. This is a 2006 Optare Tempo of Arriva's Yorkshire-based operation Yorkshire Tiger. This is seen at the 2019 Showbus rally held at Redbourn, Herts. The tigers inside are not the crew or trainees!

Stagecoach sold their London operations to Australian investment group Macquarie Bank in 2006 and then bought them back in 2010. Macquarie Bank traded as the East London Bus Company and among the buses they bought was a batch of Optare Versas in 2009. Seven years later, No. 25304 had become a permanent trainer and was on display at an Open Day held at Stratford garage on 23 July 2016.

Even examples of the Alexander Dennis Dart SLF, with the Enviro 200 body introduced in 2006, are now being taken out of frontline service and adapted as trainers. Stagecoach South 22742 was entered at the 2019 Alton Rally.

Go-Ahead London bought a batch of Mercedes Benz Citaro buses in 2009 for the Red Arrow routes 507 and 521. When these were replaced by BYD electric buses, some of the Citaros were redeployed to other bus routes, but some others became permanent trainers. One of these, MEC28 was recorded in Woolwich during October 2019. An instructor can be seen standing alongside the driver.

Bibliography

PSV Circle, *Preserved Buses 2018* (8th Ed.), (Barking, The PSV Circle, 2018)

Various fleet lists over the years published by the PSV Circle, Ian Allan, Capital Transport, LOTS etc.